First World War
and Army of Occupation
War Diary
France, Belgium and Germany

58 DIVISION
Headquarters, Branches and Services
Commander Royal Engineers
1 September 1915 - 31 January 1916

WO95/2994/1

The Naval & Military Press Ltd
www.nmarchive.com
Published in association with The National Archives

Published by

The Naval & Military Press Ltd

Unit 10 Ridgewood Industrial Park,

Uckfield, East Sussex,

TN22 5QE England

Tel: +44 (0) 1825 749494

www.naval-military-press.com

www.nmarchive.com

This diary has been reprinted in facsimile from the original. Any imperfections are inevitably reproduced and the quality may fall short of modern type and cartographic standards.

© **Crown Copyright**
Images reproduced by permission of The National Archives, London, England, 2015.

Contents

Document type	Place/Title	Date From	Date To
Heading	WO95/2994/1		
Heading	58 Division (2/1 London Div) C R E 1915 Sep-1916 Feb		
Miscellaneous	August, 1915.	01/09/1915	01/09/1915
Miscellaneous	Monthly Statement In Connection With War Diary.	01/09/1915	01/09/1915
War Diary	Wickham Market	01/09/1915	30/09/1915
War Diary	Wickham-Market Needham-Market	02/10/1915	02/10/1915
War Diary	Needham Market	28/12/1915	31/01/1916

WO 95/2994/1

58 DIVISION
(2/1 LONDON DIV)

C.R.E

1915 SEP — 1916 FEB

AUGUST, 1915.
****

UNIT.................... Hqrs, 58th (London) Divl. R.E.
DIVISION................ 58th (London) Division.
Mobilisation Centre ..... Bethnal Green, London.
Temporary War Station.... Pirbright.
Stations since occupied.. Crowborough, Bury St Edmunds, Ingham and Wickham Market.

Training.. (d).......... Has progressed satisfactorily. The move of the 2/1st Field Coy. naturally has interfered with the training of this Coy.

Discipline.. (e)........ Good

Administration..(f)...... The great length of time taken to get Officers Gazetted, promoted or transferred from London District is a cause of great trouble & interferes seriously with the training.

Organisation............ My command appears to be very unfortunate in this respect

The Home Service men being still paid, fed, &c. by us, causes an enormous amount of clerical work. It is of the utmost importance that other arrangements should be completed, as altho' responsible, O's C. Coy. have no control

Geo. W. Walters
Lt. Colonel, R.E. (T.F.)
C.R.E., 58th (London) Division.

Wickham Market.
1/9/15.

Monthly Statement in Connection with War Diary.

Unit.	2/1st. London Field Coy. R.E. (T.F).
Brigade.	2/1st. 58th (London) Divisional Engineers.
Division.	2/1st. 58th (London) Division.
Mobilization Centre.	LONDON. 10 Victoria Park Square E.
Temporary War Station.	MAIDSTONE. KENT. 4/1/15 to 21/2/15.
Stations since occupied subsequent to Concentration.	CROWBOROUGH. 22/2/15 " 27/3/15.
	BRIGHTLINGSEA. 28/3/15 " 23/4/15.
	CROWBOROUGH. 24/4/15 " 21/5/15.
	BURY ST. EDMUNDS. 22/5/15 " 16/6/15.
	INGHAM, SUFFOLK. 17/6/15 - 14/8/15
	WICKHAM MARKET 15/8/15

(g)
Reorganization of T.F. into Home & Imperial Service.

As the Home Service men have now been detached for a considerable time it is very desirable that they should be paid, fed, clothed, etc as soon as possible by the units in which they are serving. If this is for any reason impossible at present they should be transferred to the Administrative Centre.

O W B Johnstone
MAJOR R.E. (T.F.)
O/C 2/1st LONDON FIELD COY R.E. (T.F.)

1/9/15.

Army Form C. 2118.

WAR DIARY
INTELLIGENCE SUMMARY.
(Erase heading not required.)

Hour, Date, Place	Summary of Events and Information	Remarks and references to Appendices
Sept. 1st = 10ⁿᵈ Ezelheim Markt	Routine	
" 8ᵗʰ	"	Photo
" 9ᵗʰ	" Paraded 9.45 p.m. for Jyffalin. road	Photo
" 10ᵗʰ	" 9.25 p.m.	Photo
" 11ᵗʰ	"	G.S.O
" 12ᵗʰ	" learned for Jyffalin	Photo
" 13ᵗʰ	" Jyffalin farm closed 11.55 a.m.	Photo
" 14ᵗʰ	" A.D.B. inspected houses	Photo
" 15ᵗʰ	" Paraded for Jyffalin	Photo
" 16ᵗʰ/23ʳᵈ	" Destroyed three Jyffalin farms at Ruchmore	Photo
" 24ᵗʰ	" Attended the attack at Hay-day Farm on the Earthworks.	Photo
" 25ᵗʰ/27ᵗʰ	Routine	Photo
" 28ᵗʰ	The G.O.C. 69ᵗʰ Division attended a Conference with regard to the	Photo
"	Defensive Posts on River of afterwards inspected the Position	Photo
"	occupied by the 145ᵗʰ Infantry Brigade	Photo
" 29ᵗʰ/30ᵗʰ	" Routine	Photo

No 6 Cheshire Regt
Bgde 58ᵗʰ (Garrison) Division
1/10/15

Army Form C. 2118.

WAR DIARY
INTELLIGENCE SUMMARY.
(Erase heading not required.)

Instructions regarding War Diaries and Intelligence Summaries are contained in F. S. Regs., Part II. and the Staff Manual respectively. Title pages will be prepared in manuscript.

Hour, Date, Place	Summary of Events and Information	Remarks and references to Appendices
1915 October 2nd WICKHAM-MARKET NEEDHAM-MARKET	Moved by road from Wickham Market to Needham Market with the 2/1st & 2/2nd London Field Coys. R.E.	H.Q. 58th (London) Divisional R.E. [stamp: 58th (LONDON) DIVISION 3 NOV 1915 GENERAL STAFF] A.G.B. Geo. G. Walters Lt. C.R.E. 58th (London) Division 2/11/15

Army Form C. 2118.

WAR DIARY
or
INTELLIGENCE SUMMARY.

(Erase heading not required.)

G.S. 58th (London) Division al RE.

Instructions regarding War Diaries and Intelligence
Summaries are contained in F. S. Regs., Part II.
and the Staff Manual respectively. Title pages
will be prepared in manuscript.

Hour, Date, Place	Summary of Events and Information	Remarks and references to Appendices
1915 November Needham Market	[signature]	P.6.6.
	Geo. C. Colvin Lt. Col. R.E. St CRE. 58th (London) Division	

[Stamp: 58th LONDON DIVISION 3 DEC 1915 GENERAL STAFF]

WAR DIARY or INTELLIGENCE SUMMARY.

Army Form C. 2118.

CRE

H.Q. 58th (London) Divisional RE

Hour, Date, Place	Summary of Events and Information	Remarks and references to Appendices
NEEDHAM MARKET 28/12/15	Lieut-Col G.W. WALTERS C.R.E. proceeds to SOUTHAMPTON for Staff Tour overseas	(OTW) O.W. Johnstone Major RE (TF) O.C. 2/1st London Field Coy RE (TF) a/ C.R.E.

Army Form C. 2118.

WAR DIARY
or
INTELLIGENCE SUMMARY.

(Erase heading not required.)

C.E. 58th Divisional Engineers

Instructions regarding War Diaries and Intelligence Summaries are contained in F. S. Regs., Part II. and the Staff Manual respectively. Title pages will be prepared in manuscript.

Hour, Date, Place	Summary of Events and Information	Remarks and references to Appendices
NEEDHAM MARKET 1/1/16 to 31/1/16	nil	G.C.W.
	Geo. C. Walters Lt. Col. R.E. T.F. C.R.E. 58th (London) Divn	

[Stamp: 58th (LONDON) DIVISION — 3 FEB 1916 — GENERAL STAFF]

www.ingramcontent.com/pod-product-compliance
Lightning Source LLC
Chambersburg PA
CBHW081515160426
43193CB00014B/2697